Right Now, Carissima

Carissima

POEMS

Joseph Phillip Natoli

ISBN 979-8-218-30336-5

Library of Congress Control Number: 2023920643

Bad Animal Books

To Elaine

Introduction

Introductory words to the words of poems are like introductory words to a first tasting of an arancini: useless. Eat the arancini.

Over the fifty years Elaine Anne Natoli (née Tuminelli) and I were married, my response too often to a request of hers was "Right now, I'm doing. . .". Something. Whatever. Finishing a sentence. Rushing to a deadline. Forking a delectable. Those put offs are like hot pokers to my soul now that Elaine is gone, no longer visible in this world though always visible when I close my eyes. You see, there will never be a "Right now" when we are together again in any way an empiricist would accept.

In her playful way she took to mocking my put offs, my distracted absorption away from her, by declaring "Oh, excuse me! Right now, you've got a great thought, someplace so deep you can't be disturbed, on the edge of a phenomenal breakthrough maybe. I'll wait."

Truth is she far surpassed whatever I thought could exist. I never reached the depths of her own mystery. My phenomenal breakthrough came after she died: There should never have been a "Now" without her. It's as simple as that.

The mundanity that fills our lives is like all that packaging material you get with an Amazon delivery. Our lives get filled in with what I guess orders/arranges/schedules a bearable order, as if at the end of life, we look back and say "Well, I got that done without a hitch."

I filled in the days with my ways just as others do and did, right now endlessly occupied when, ironically, I was foundationally, ontologically, heart and soul occupied only by Elaine. Was I conscious of that? I was in the way a toddler in the park wanders from his Mom adventurously but not without glancing back to make sure she is still there.

I never went far from Elaine. I never went anywhere from her from the first time I saw her, though I have over the years travelled widely, many times without her. Just seeing her calmed my soul, pulled my mind from the dark affinities and imaginaries I seem always to be writing about.

Right Now, Carissima is one long elegy in many movements, some of love, loss, and grief, some of anger at every Celestial plan that requires Death. I mean plans that feature Death an essential part, even as far as leading to immortal bliss. The entire elegy is a disclosure from within the Everydayness of life of my love for Elaine.

There is a macro dimension here, an abstract universal one, call it what I called it in all my postmodernity writing: a Grand Narrative. For beyond her person and by means of it, I have come to an awakened sense that without this profound breadth and depth of love she exemplified, we would cease to exist as any form of life distinct from the artificial and robotic.

Some passages of this elegy posit no glorious After Life but simply what is given by the Departed -- a gift. This is a gift that those like Elaine who have lived no less sublimely and generously than any anointed Celestial pass on to us. We do not live within the memory of those who hate, even hate greatly. They burn out quickly like a Roman candle. They leave no counsel "to live in memory of their hate." Everything dies here and is brought to Death. I am aware that Now we are deeply buried in this reign of hatred. My mourning and this elegy surface from such.

And yet, though we are so benighted, we are not without rescue because we can live within the memory of those who awaken within us the light of their own lives. Their spirit makes possible an undeniable spiritual nature to our lives and our world. That is so because they are the substance of that spirit. No need to look up at the Heavens.

2

We know Paradise because we have seen and heard, we know those who have created such in our own lives. We live within the memory of those whose love never leaves us.

This elegy then is not sabotaged by grief, though I was over and over again overwhelmed by such, but I saw through Elaine's life what so inspired me. She seemed to have lived within this aura of the love gifted to us by the departed from the very beginning of my life with her. And though she smiled when at the very end of her life, I bemoaned not ever reaching into the heart of her mystery, I discover in these many days since her death that in that smile, the mystery was solved.

"Numinous" is the title I gave to a painting of her and done soon after she died. I believe the ineffable aura of her goes beyond the earthly but evokes not terror but awe. I was humbled by her life. I am forever in awe of her and what she left not simply to me but as a gift to our shared humanity.

In the penultimate chapter of *Time is the Fire*, a novel, there is a poem, not included in this elegy. But I think the best segue to a book of poems is a poem:

I am in a waiting room

I hear a clock ticking

The time it tells is timeless

For there are no more clocks ticking

I don't know if it will be a long time

Or if I have been there a long time

Or if I have just arrived

I don't know what or who I'm waiting for

You see, she's dead

And no matter if I wait for eons

Grow hoary and decrepit old

She will be dead

But I am waiting for her nonetheless

For you see I don't know

Where I end and she begins

Where I begin and she ends

And so will never feel

Apart

Right Now, Carissima
The idea of death fills me
As if life all along
Were a vessel now emptied
So, it's not an idea?
An emotion then?
The thing in itself?
What is it?
Go small, back away
Begin with the easy
And answerable
Do you look for me here
Living without you?
Or are you purged of me?
Beyond and ethereal
Is it still you?
Forever now a soul only?
What a great task
To be a Soul
And yet be unknown.
What lies outside
My field of vision
You now see?

I have not been as aware
As a traveler as I should be
I'm fallen
This is the true After the Fall
I didn't know what sin Eve's was
Or why we lay Death at her door
Or why I don't miss her
Why I don't mourn her
Till now with you
Daughter of Thy Fair Eve
I miss you
I miss nothing as I do you

I believe you yet watch over me
I see your presence there
As I look up
Maybe not
No longer a presence
Death made that so
Made you invisible
Voiceless
Though when I listen
I hear you
Do you hear me?
My questions tire you
Your fool such a fool
So easy to fool

I miss the issue and the point
Forsake the observable
Pick the bone
That cannot be known
Question even the flower
Examine the roots
Of the unharvested
Certainly
The reasoning why we're here

What it would be like
If you and I were
Never to be at all?
It would be as if
At the beginning
There was Nothing
Out of which evolved
Not Something
But endless Nothing
Death begins here

Not in any celestial plan

But we were something
Weren't we, Carissima?
My conception of Life
It's conceivability
Begins with you.
With you
The world has always
Lived for me
Right now, Carissima
You come to me
No Heaven worthy of you
Though I always saw
The idea of it
In you

If we grew old together
One of us did it well
And one of us froze
You couldn't afford to freeze
You had to give life
Twice
And nurture both
You loved the movie
Being There
I wasn't
One of us saw
What was there to be done
And did it
When these cancers
Came at you
Like ferocious waves to the shore
You drew from within a steady course
That does not rave
Against an end you clearly see
But like yet another wave
That pounds unexpected
You face with valor
Indomitable warrior
In your eyes
Right now
A fading lightness
This gentle leaving of you
I cannot speak
Oh, I am in awe of you
A gift finer than
Any Heaven could give
So far beyond
What I ever deserved
Right now, Carissima
Time is painfully sad
For me

Overwhelmed by what
I failed to see
You would give forgiveness
I know
You meet me too
As you always have
In your private way
Of reaching my heart
If I was less than I should have been
You never said
Never right now
Be better
You never said

Right now
I think it best
All the questions that come to mind
Didn't come then
I wasn't ready
Nor ever will be
What purpose or part
In a Divine Plan your death
Served
I will never be ready
To hear
You are gone
To haunt dreams and memories
Always dead
Can never be right
Or ever will be
No exculpatory case
Can ever be won
The physics of it
Never true
The biology of Death
A futile pursuit
Who ordered the ways of dying?
Who ordered this Autopsy?
The theogony miscast
The rituals unredeeming
I stand without need of grace
Though they knock
"Do you know the Bible?"
Seigneur, I yield my time
But never yours
What you expect of me
I know
I must bend
To live beyond you
I am right now

Not ready
Nor ever will be

Right now
Someone is telling me
You're gone
Abbandonata. You?
I take offense
Are you gone
When you are no longer remembered?
When everyone who knew you now gone?
What joy in that
You be alive only in memory?
A shaky ground
A diminishing abyss
To lay my life upon?
What grief lasts here
Where Time burns
It all down?
Perhaps Life is other
Than what anyone knows
The Now never again Now
Always only Then
And you're not gone
How can anyone know
Death other than this?
Except it was never present
That you, Carissima
Were never there
At all
Flourishing beyond
What I could imagine
Surely in a realm
Death cannot reach
Cannot reap the brightness
It can never see
Cannot remember
What it never knew

As the Moon draws the tide
The noise and motion of the days
Draw me away from you
Though they cannot
I am at low ebb
Vacated like the sand
When the wave is gone
Might you come back to me
Find me on the shore
Waiting for you
A wind rushing to me
I see us as one again
Together
And then I can't
You are so far ahead of me
Death is a tough barrier
A wall I cannot scale
You've gone to mist I cannot touch
Where am I going without you?
Up and down there and back
All paths lead nowhere
But in my mind I find you
Behind schedule I find you
You are so far ahead of me
I cannot see if it's you
But the wind rushing to me
How many hours and days
Months and years
You are so far ahead of me
Where I can no longer find you

I see all signs of you on this road
That Eve never died
Nor Adam ever cried
They are
And you

Right now
Beyond the mysteries
The gods would know
Silent the Angels
Though they watch
When you go

Miraculous Chance
Us finding us
Meeting beyond
The reach of anyone's reach
There was always a mystique
To you
Beyond what the mind or body
Can say or know
If there was a plan
I never knew it
A silent gaze you give me
In the end
I think this life
Is true for me
Because you made it so
I think the journey
Was fabled
Before Time was called
Particles co-joined
And Chance was cast

Though I grow older alone and die
It does not matter
For two who were once together
On a journey on a boat
On a plane
On a train
On a Pullman
On the back of a dragon
When Time is no more
It does not matter
My death is not an opportunity
To see you again
Be with you again
Death gives me no pass
Through the Gates of Eden
Outside as I am
I think in so many eons ahead
You and I will fill the world
With the atoms we once were
I the muddy soil
Far from a lovely bower
You the stunning flower

"Death, therefore, the most awful of evils, is nothing to us, seeing that, when we are, death is not come, and, when death is come, we are not."
– Epicurus

There's a landscape of fever
    To Death
    A mixed tape of dream
Nightmare too
A ramble in woods
Lost from the path
A time before you
This time after
My knowing now
Like a god's
My knowing now
Of every place you ever were
In every moment
From the beginning
Never not you

Right now
It is morning
You are rising
Later on you will climb
The stairs
"I'm going to take my shower"
You tell me
It's yours
You possess your shower
Hold onto it
A ritual that ties time
Together for you
Yet a moment out of time
Your own private Sabbath
The way you tend to your body
This is a careful attention
To Being
In your well-made world
Without any celestial ambition
All promised paths to perfection
Humbled by your humility
"This woman is perfect
In every way"
Your doctor writes
A memorial service testament
I eschew the invitations
To let those happen
Obscure your words I hear
"I'm going to take my death
Quietly and privately
Now"

She comes to me
Though I hear them
Carry her body down the stairs
She hears it too
No, we don't want
A last viewing
She comes to me
Taking me to where she is
From the very beginning
We took the road less traveled by
She comes to me
An empty bowl left in the sink
So she makes me laugh
She comes to me
All reasoning against it
Except all my reasons lie in her
She comes to me
When I so yearn for her
Is this what you want?
Oh, God, yes it is
She comes to me
How I ask because
You've never gone
Such a mystery she says and laughs.
She comes to me
Though I fear a dying
My own to come
She reaches back a hand
Come to me
She comes to me.

Some dreams I've had
Before beginning
After the end
Sitting in the sun
Already seeing
What's not there
Hearing what is silent
Time that never was
She looks up
In her mouth
A cut of dark peat
Is this Death?
A *memento mori*?
Less lovely than Aphrodite
Surfing a clam shell
Something here, Carissima,
You tell me
I am not ready to know

I get that feeling of being alone
My former days and ways by all unknown
My habits a vexation like the loose ways
Of an old dog on a carpet or a straggly parrot
Whose repetitions are no longer amusing
It's not difficult now
To see a time when I am no more
But it's hard
Though not in any way we can know
The way absence is nothing
When nothing was present before
As now you come to the door
And the world comes to sense
Though I am a fool before it
Though thirsty
A brush stroke to the canvas
Sails to the wind
Quixote to his quest
A drunken head on a pillow to rest
A frolic into an incoming surf
A wood fire taking an igniting breath
I cross the Pyrenees as Roland did
Hoping to find you
Though I am a fool

Right now
It's clear to me
There was little of me
Before you
And always too much
This love for you
So much less your preference
I think with me it was
This love for you
So easily led astray
That somehow what I could do
And display or prove to all
Would mean more than
This love for you
I see my own celestial reckoning
Being made
"Blindness" the verdict
To your devotion and commitment
I make no defense beyond
This love for you
Seigneur, I yield my time
But what reckoning of you?
What are its credentials?
What authority is behind the screen?
Why bring to an end
What cannot end
This love for you
Why end a life when all that has been tilled
Is ready to harvest?
What plan is there
In shadowing a life with cancer?
Are we learning some lesson here?
Am I closer to an Eternal Reward
When I accept a defense
A rationale
An alibi for your death?

This anger of mine
Dies in the warm light of you
Cannot hold on against
This love for you
Lost within your gaze
I am embraced and linger
Frozen at the moment
Of your dying
Forever hearing your laugh
You had no plan
As to what life meant
Nor care as to what Death
Would do with you
I am blind and fearful
So angry by this abandon
So incapable without you
Drunk with
This love for you
Who knows the strength
Of your own light
The whole cause and career
Of our Being
I would know
Oh, I am grateful beyond any knowing
In this
This love for you

Her beauty beyond being told
Her body comes at me in waves
I have no hope of oxygen
I sink to the ocean floor
She's a dream I cannot fulfill
A mystery I cannot say or paint
Then reach out all hands to her
She's all of the tide rolling
All sister to the Sun
All now adrift in the Stars
Who could be without her
If all this were true?

Right now
    All the life and times
    Of 60th Street Brooklyn
New Utrecht Avenue the corner
Are shuttered away
The world moves on
Like a perpetual motion machine
Unmoved
The mindless Everydayness
That should just stop
Doesn't
The callous Mundanity
Unmoved by your departure
That went on
Though some didn't know
You were ill or fatally ill
Or suddenly to die
In the middle of their day at the lake
Unplanned in their lives
Not on their calendars
Your Death
An Emergency call
"She's already cold" he says
Knowing as a routine
Death's coldness
And how it feels
Knowing as a routine
It's not his own death he feels
How much I am angered
By this disrespect
How much I am angered
By the world not stopping
When you stopped
I cannot express
It's a tragic flaw in me
The Divine Plan

I cannot recognize
The economics of ambitious mortality
The theogony of hopeful immortality
No
What anything ever meant to me
Rests in you
No end to this
What Heaven is proposed to be
Was here already in you

How much is gone
Now that you're gone
It's impossible to say
So much of you to feel
Everywhere in this house
You made
As I sit here
This home your voice
Moving as you move
The memory in things
The awesomeness of that
What you put your hand to
It's this puppet by your chair
Tells me solemnly
"I'm giving my life to you"
I tell you it's too great a gift
My gratitude rides on the back
Of a comet
Forever circling this planet
Forever alive within your gaze

I suppose if you've now discovered
After your dying
So small we are in this mortal flight
But the plan
Of Creation, Fall, Redemption, Salvation
Re-creation in other form
Some purpose you were to fulfill
You would I know be charitable
And forgive the Divine its presumption
In assuming you would take part
But the plan
You have is different
You would I know fill the Void
Laugh Oblivion into good form
Look into the Abyss
Free the fears therein
Conjure beyond wizardry
Re-seat the Angels
Benched and old
Fulfill more than the gods could imagine
Before time was born
And stories told

Right now, Carissima
I'm in your garden
I will put a memory stone
Elaine's Garden
There's a mystery rose tree
Planted when and by whom
I don't know
Years before the sun
Came through a corridor
And found us
Now roses bloom
In long cycles until late Fall
The botany is not right
For when all is dying
Or dead
There are still roses
Greeting you in the morning light
Which strikes a bench close by
And on that bench I see you
The physics is not right
In the fading autumn sun
Surrounding you
Like the finest brush work
Silent you sit
In your garden
Though
The biology is not right
Your hair grown silver
"Hollywood hair" I say to you
You want no part of that
Stage I would put you upon
I will never go back on my words
That the beauty of you
The soft and gentle and profound
Beauty of you
No religion has ever been right

I could never write what I knew about you
You didn't make it easy
Knowing you
Preferring silence to words
Mystery to declaration
You were right
The greater you love
The less to be said
No telling of what is true
And yet without that
What could we ever do?
Time now is the fire
In which I burn
To see beyond your mystery
There now with Death's
Own mystery
I struggle
My forever devotion
Futile and foolish
I should go on with my life
What did I ever do
That now I could do that?
Take a new turn
As if you never were?
When I find you there
An oil painting perhaps
Where the movement of color and shape
Some lines mimicking something
A flat gestalt of mood and world
Of something personal about you
By a chance stroke
If my luck is good
Perhaps not
Yet, the way the paint advances
Easily
Or retards the mission of the hand

Belays the purpose of what sails
Furiously and desperately
The artist's mind sets
Close-hauled against the winds
Of intent and ambition
Something though
Trying to reach you
What did I ever do
That now I could do that?
Know you, Elaine, as you are
In yourself alone
The mystery of yourself
You own for eternity, Carissima

Right now
It's as it has always been
A matter of making sense
Of Death
Our cleverness here
Our inventiveness
Sharp eye for benefit
Is unsurpassed in the galaxy
Where it seems Death
Has already happened
Or Life has never begun
A man on the Moon
Is nothing in achievement
Compared to a man
Who rises from Death
For all our benefit
If certain conditions are met
After all resurrection to Life
Cannot be a handout
You can't live reckless
Of other lives
Or destroy your own
Devour their unceasing pain
To quench your self-love
Go Heavenward immortalized
Alongside the lives you've wrecked
Including your own
Some calibration of worth
Measurement of good and evil
Though no one dies faultless
The vices and virtues
So braided in us
At best only a partial resurrection
A partial condemnation
A flowing in and out
Of Heaven and Hell

My life is a Forever Parole
No life condemns itself
No one knows where the guilt lies
In themselves
Though easily seen in others
Right now, Carissima
I live in the light of you
Of those who loved truly
And endlessly beyond themselves
Overflowing spirits
Replenishment of the world
Eternal Faith born
In the way we love
In no After World
But
Right now, Carissima

When I see you you're not there
I make a meal to share
But you stand me up
I leave a poem on your pillow
Carve our names in this dappled willow
I leave signs and omens everywhere
I reach out beyond what I can bear
This is something that can be changed
A temporary absence before return
So much evidence for this
If the void were eternal
There would be no beer and burgers
The Cubs would never win
The dust of the Earth
Belong only to the Dead
I leave these words
Some quality of Being
Emerging from mind and body
But not of them
An awareness without fear
Of Death
A love that holds the world
Together
But you stand me up

Right now, Carissima
You surely know
We would have added up
The parts differently
I mean the value of each
How deeply one thing
Or another
Would sink in
Root in memory
Or drift beyond recall
It is what it is
Though not with us

We would name the chapters
Of our lives differently
Some of mine not existing
In yours
Some of yours not present at all
In mine
A beginning is hard to find
Though not with us

A Genesis ours
Equally wrapped in mythic mystery
Miracles too
That we became a "thing"
You and I
We could easily have missed
Each other
Gone the other way
Like wayward quanta
Who never have to meet
Like a Cosmos
That never had to be
Though not with us

A something to us
Where you would be
So would I
The beginning of you
The beginning of me
An ending somewhere
Though not with us

I hear the sound of your car
Black Honda
I'm out of bed by the window
Watch as you drive up the Court
Stop briefly signal turn
And go on
Out of my sight
I wait until I can no longer
Hear you
The sound of you
This leaving
A rehearsal I fear

I am at the kitchen door
You stand by the coffee machine
Mister Coffee
Your blue Cozy
Your bare feet in black fuzzies
The birds you feed
Fussing at the feeder
I see the Charm
That makes the world
For me

I turn and look up from my work
In the garden
You stand there on the deck
How long you've been there
I don't know
But now you have it
"I'm going now," you call to me
"Okay," I call back.
Never ever wanting you to go
Never quite reading
The Signs of Eternity

R
　ight now
　I'm where you left me
　But Where?

Some place you and I
Have already been
Maybe it's the Mountain Top Inn
"Hi, Kids," Mrs. Angeloni greets us
The Catskill Game Farm
No longer there
Derelict
Except we're always there

Maybe it's the summer
Home in Amherst
The Oaks in Henniker
"The Only Henniker on Earth"
Hatch House and the puppies
We go back and look for it
But it's burned down
The forest has already taken
The Where it was

Then on Ballston Lake
The ice skating cabinette
We both falling toward
Each other on the ice
The retreat to Brooklyn
No longer knowing
Where

We are a family
Amelia Mary, you and me
Dickens and Cissy
Our turtles
Extracted like a tooth

From a Where we were
There's a magic to us
You conjure beyond Time and Space
We are in flight
On the carpet you make
Where
Is everywhere

In the "Big Camper"
To Oxley Holl'er
To a new baby, Brenda Lillian
This Where is an older century
We are in
You do it all as well
As any pioneer woman
I never know how we survive
It all goes deeper
Than I could know

The thing is
Never the thing
The Where doesn't seem to settle
Nothing evens out
No place lands
Except you make it so
Windsor Forest Red Rock
Other Wheres
The road ends
It's a dead end
Baldwin Court

You are dead here
In this house
This is Where
It ends for you

Right now I am harbored
In the womb you made
For all of us
As if you knew from the start
You could create life
In so many ways
In so many ways, Carissima
I cannot count
Where and how and when
Over time what was ever there
Was you
There because of you
Without all falls to ruin

I am in awe of you
The Where like the years
No longer matter
Except what is you
Left in all of us
No words to say goodbye
To one
Always here
Right now
Where

I never will know you
Your full presence
Don't ask me why
Unless I be blind
Without prophecy
Unless I be deaf
To silence
Unless I be out of sync
Shallow diver
Into the deep pulse and bones
Of things
Distracted on the banks
Of the fast running
Sad brevity of being
But for all this
I hold on to you
Oh, silent wondrous center
Of my life

Right now
We're at *L'Argent Main*
In Quebec
We're young
Just married
The restaurant is closed
And we are so disappointed
That the owner opens it for us

We are young
And you are lit up

With primordial embers of Being
In the wine
The giving of the Sun
Its miraculous reception by the grass
The gravity of Heaven's incomprehensible silence
The most certain promise of Life

You are young
Lit up with it

Without this knowing anything
Out of time
Nil the intent
Laughable the choices
Compress the everyday
Into a noisy tableau

Except you are young
Lit up with it

Whether you are now someplace not a place
Waiting for me in some timeless time
I cannot testify to any Grand Inquisitor
But I see you now
Slipping into dark waters
Like a dreamer into a dream
Unafraid
A voyager
On a boat at sea
All accommodations made
On a boat at sea
The sails set
On a boat at sea

I'm advised to seek
A grievance consigliere
To impress upon me that
You are not here
That for you there is no Now
Or When or Then
Or ever will be again
I'm to understand this
That When is Now
And you're dead

I'm dead to all that

What miserable advice is this
That your Death is in the way
Of my going forward
Of my returning to a living
Where my grief no longer
Fills the room
Abuses the public
With my private grief

Why not live in the memory
Of you and call that
My only life?
Isn't there an entire religion
Living in memory of One dead?
Instructed for the sake
Of their souls to do so?

I prefer not to
Bring to an end
What Death marks as an end
Or live as advised to move on
When I would love you
As faithfully dead

As alive to me

No understanding reaches me
I leave my understanding
Like a worn out t-shirt
On a rail station bench
On a grief journey

Grander stuff than what
We can understand
Saturates the world
There is no time to move on
When time ends
It's different Then
When there is no
When or Then
It's where you are

You alone would stand in awe
If the squeezles knew more than geese
While the holy fakirs screech
Farther than bits can reach

All unspoiled by lobbyist
You alone would stand in awe
If all the Lower Orders
Heard beyond this town's borders

Gave lessons none attended
The College of Pretended
You alone would stand in awe
At the wisdom of the boar

Such a life never deposed
By what idiots proposed
Blind to any Chain of Law
You alone would stand in awe

Right now
It's 4:20
You've died
I wait
For that respectful moment
A gesture of the Cosmos
But that doesn't happen
There is no break
In the momentum of the Everyday
Though I remain
Stopped
Transfixed
Forever caught
Right now
You died
I am a useless bystander
The morality of anything
Turned upside down
Sanctity cast aside
By the play of Chance
It all clatters and chatters
Around me
And will until I die
Right now
I am still
Gazing at you
Finally returning your gaze
Your hand pointing to my heart
The mystery of you
So present to me
Goes beyond
My survival in sadness
Such sadness never true
To how you laughed
Carissima

Make this ball of life an eternal thing
Where worms crawl bees work and cardinals wing
Unburden ev'ry woman from ordeal
Make knowing always entry to what's real
Cast all love free of tortured simile
Make the root of things a vibrant flower
Inverse the dusty rooms of staid power
Open eyes to the imagine of sleep
Let Infinity mock what words would keep
Make this ball of life an eternal thing
Confound the sacred Celestial said
And so awaken by magic the Dead

Right now, Carissima
I'm wandering
Wondering
Like a dream I once had
Waiting for you
When you for so long
You had gone away
Like a dream I once had
Before dawn
When I move quietly
So that the living do not waken
Or the Dead do not pass on
This passage of you from me
Like a dream I once had
This terrible goodbye
When you hold me
When no one can
When we were for a time
Like a dream I once had

I'm in the garden at the hottest time of day
I'm alert to sounds now
Trying to get an attention
Though bewildered
I look into a clear blue sky
Stately spruce and flourishing greenery
The travails of cloud
So there you are I say to myself
In the beauty of this garden
Beneath the roof of Angels
I stop and rest here
For how long
As yet to be written

Right now, Carissima
We are down in Oxley Holl'er
You tell me it's time to go
To the Princeton Hospital
Yesterday you had fit a window
Into its frame
You fit it perfectly
You had a baby later
You did it perfectly
It's what you do
This perfection in you
Right now
You are looking at me
Face flushed
I'm alright you tell me
A dew of that labor
Of birth radiates you
There has never been
For me a grander sight
I don't know what messages
Eternity sends
Though this is one
This perfection in you
I don't know how it's done
In Heaven
But here I see and know it
This perfection in you

Just by chance
We are here
Just by chance
We see
Though we cannot see what is there
Or say what is
Bound we think by choice
Though we are thrown
Like a pot on a wheel
Just by chance
We wake up
Is this what Death is for?
What forgiveness
Opens the eyes of the blind and dumb?
I would be dumb for eternity
Rather than you die
There is no purpose in Death
Or excuses in Heaven
We reason in the shallow grave
Of what we think
And thought
Just by chance
Our lives were not savaged
By club or spear or arrow
Our souls plundered
By pagan gods
Just by chance, Carissima
Our time always the perfect time
The time
We lived beyond knowing
Just by chance
There was you and I
When outrageous fortune
Let us be
Together
Just by chance

Right now
You're getting ready for bed
You're banking the fire
In the kitchen stove
In the morning there are embers
Glowing
Easily brought to flame
The breath of you fills the house
The light the heat
You keep us all alive
I never quite see your competence
Now I see your life was a gift
You tended
In trust for us all
So much questionable
You would not question
I am busy in forgettable fields
You're banking the fire
But I am never there
What did it mean?
Where's the harvest
When the fire goes out?
You're banking the fire
The low murmur of the wood burning
Embers glowing
Never dying
Right now, Carissima

I finish the sauce off with Marsala *fino*
The orange cat sinews out of the garage
Death puts the king and the pawn in the same box
And of these neighbors what can I say?
Nothing said Now
Means anything to me
I'm a little short this month he tells her
Cut the plexi-glass to fit, please
That one is in love with her phone
Tell me, Joe
How do you get a Big Bang out of a thick soup?
I don't
Maybe I'll remember what was said
Remember more surely
What was never said
In Time
I'll see you before I leave or you go
Keep all the doors unlocked
Nothing little can mask this day
When you slip away

Hard to see what was young and fresh
The smoothness of skin
And all tautness gone
The tightness of muscle falling to gravity
The quick recall
A taunting absence
Hard to know how mortality
Springs upon us so suddenly
An ambush promised at birth
But never expected
Every part loses its shine and bleaches or greys
The pigments laid one upon the other
In the long pursuit of a likeness
To what we once were
So hard to disguise the parting
The slow creep of darkness into day
The futile pursuit of what leaves
The reach toward what might stay

Right now
When I see you dance
You're listening to Dion
The Supremes Streisand
Dinah Washington
Keb Mo
Freda Payne *Band of Gold*
Georgia sung by Freddy
Jerome Sweets Kerry
Second Nature
Pete & Steve
Blues Luncheons
Play *Mississippi Queen*
The Lash
Smooth DaDa
Stanley Craig
Rob "Pay my money down"
Kevin Bobby Jeff
In *Mort's*
When I see you dance
NYC schoolyard
Your body feels the beat
I watch and try to move
In sync
Never quite there
The Dancer from the Dance
The Life from the Death
The sounds of Always
Never quite there
When I see you dance

You are holding up yours arms
I can lift you out and beyond
Death
But you cannot stand
I lay you back on the bed
No sounds of distress
You seem so at peace
As if you trusted
Death taking you
You die silently though I call and call
This is our parting
I hear the words of my Faith
"Till death do you part"
I bend no knee now
I subscribe to no celestial plan
Requiring the services
Of Death
I carry so much of what you are to me
Inside me now that I am bewildered
In everything I do as if I too
Am some place I do not know
There is something that never ends
Where every memory begins
Where the time I am walking to 60th Street
To find you so young waiting for me
Now looking into my eyes telling me something
Wordlessly that I cannot grasp
"I'll be gone for a while."

R ight now
We're waiting for Larry
Returning from Boston
Bringing ocean trout and wine
To The Oaks
On Colby Hill Road
To Hatch House
On Bear Hill Road
This is where we live

We're waiting for Troy and Tom
An old pickup coming down
Oxley Holl'er Road
Coming to wire the house
Rev. Callier to find us water
Mr. Parker's Franklin Stove
All the wood to heat
This is how we live

Right now
I'm waiting for you
Your car coming down
Baldwin Court
Swinging sharply into the drive
Wide turn into the garage
This is the place Now
This is When

So
I studied the numbers and counted my age
Studied the Lord's words and spelled my name
Took one part and another on the stage
So
I studied Vico and the *Book of Job*
Looked in a mirror and saw no one there
Played mad Hamlet with fitful manic flare
So
I followed the traces that went before
Saw Blake singing as his life slipped away
Shut off your mortality like a door
So
I painted canvases of boats and sails
Painted you lovely in the house you made
Counted the flow of years and marked them paid
So
I studied closely what I could not leave
Traced your face back to the Garden and Eve

As if this were a given thing
Your love for me
All something that is
But as easily could not be
So curious this dream
I expect a rekening
In Dutch the bill to be paid
So curious this feeling
Somehow I think
We could never hold
As we did
So curious this love
Inseparable
As we were
I fear the scenario of a better me
I could not write
Nor would you buy
So curious this fear
But why change the course
We took?
Oh, I cannot write
To make others see
What you saw in me
Or I in you
So very curious these lines
Though here I try

We are emptied now
As when light leaves a star
Three thousand light years away
Never distant
Loss not there but here
The Void not there but here
Where the darkness of Death
Thickens the mind in a mire
Then no way out
No rewind
Reckless wandering imploding
But if there was no origin to you
We could presume to know
So like the incalculable of the Heavens
The arcane Order of Angels
The mystique of the Sun's power
No need in your life for an ending
Begun in wondrous mystery
Into a long precession
Of days we cannot order
A Natural World yet of mist
We are of unknowable stuff
How could we know an ending
When surely the beginning of you
Went on before

Right now
We've pulled The Big Camper
Off to the side of the road
You make sandwiches
At the small table
In the distance I see
An Amish symbol on a worn red barn
I have no idea what it means
To ward off evil and bring good fortune
Or where we are going
Where does evil enter
And good fortune brought?
But I have fears
Right now
We've pulled The Big Camper
Off to the side of the road
You make sandwiches
At a small table
What I see in your face
I cannot know the meaning
And then I do

There are in our existence spots of time,
That with distinct pre-eminence retain
A renovating virtue, whence--depressed
By false opinion and contentious thought,
Or aught of heavier or more deadly weight,
In trivial occupations, and the round
Of ordinary intercourse--our minds
Are nourished and invisibly repaired;
A virtue, by which pleasure is enhanced,
That penetrates, enables us to mount,
When high, more high, and lifts us up when fallen.
This efficacious spirit chiefly lurks
Among those passages of life that give
Profoundest knowledge to what point, and how,
The mind is lord and master--outward sense
The obedient servant of her will. Such moments
Are scattered everywhere, taking their date
From our first childhood.

Wordsworth, *The Prelude*, XII, 1805

Who's to choose among fifty years spots of time
That renovate a world you've left?
There's a chaos to each day
Offering us a different face
A different reasoning to what we know
Nor revealing in the end what life is for
Nor something missed time makes dearer
So stunned by epiphanies
These puns of yours that spark by surprise
Mounting beyond where memory lies

Right now we're sitting
     At a vintage kitchen table
     Foldable leaves
Watching a retro toaster toast
The Toast
The Oaks New Hampshire
Our third Chez Maison
After our Amherst summer home
And our Colonie cabin
The sides of this toaster
Fall down
You lay the slices in
Close it
Plug
Wait for
The Toast
We sit and watch
Judging when
The Toast
Is done by the smell
Unnerving this
The coils go red hot
Done
Unplug
We do it again
Laughing
We make more of this
The Toast
Right now, Carissima

In all my days
I am led to you
When I roll over and find a fresh side
And feel an easeful comfort as you go deeper into sleep
I am led to you
When I throw your pack up on a ride at 6
From Amsterdam and later climb down
Into a sunny day at the Gare du Nord
I am led to you
When I find off the trail and behind bushes
Water on the *Camino* and I can drink in shade
I am led to you
When I sit among friends and listen
And then think of the book by my bed
I am led to you
When I stand in the *Calle in* Donostia waiting
And then the old cook motions me to a table
I am led to you
When it's the last day of school and I rush out
Into days of a summer I cannot foresee
I am led to you
When I join friends along 11th Avenue at Christmas
And hear Christmas music from the shops
I am led to you
When my mother touches with a cool hand
My head to feel my fever and I sleep
I am led to you
When I sit with you at the campfire
Devouring a horde of butter cookies you've made
I am led to you
When I see a smiling face walking toward me
As I return from my first day of teaching
I am led to you
When I wake and find you gone
I am led to you

Right now
You're at the table
Hatch House
New Hampshire
Giving Amelia an egg
Out of a tiny Gerber jar
Dickens and Cissy
Lying near
Alert to the possibility
Of fallen bits
Amelia crawls about
Canine accompanied
Gleeful as she pulls pots
Out of a cabinet
So we call her Pep
Nothing diminishes
After you're gone
But the little rolls upward
Becomes a twister
Its significance other worldly
Now
Right now
You're sitting in the oak rocker
In Oxley Holl'er
Holding close Brenda only days old
She will not let you go
We call her Buns
Nothing diminishes
After you're gone
I hear the voices
And the peals of thunder
I break the seals
Of Life and Death
I see your face

You'll not be here for this, Carissima
But you miss nothing I think
When an elegy
Is not wanted at all

Right now
I see you sitting
Across from me
"Please," you say
So softly a plea
So much in your eyes
As in your drift to death
To let you go
This is a time before
That if you would eat
You would live
I cannot hold this need I have
For you to live
I cannot hold the demand
As always you know better
Than I
This need I have
For you to live
For you to keep your strength
Never to fade
Never to be lost to me
And you would do it for me
Knowing this need I have
For you to live
It can't be done
There are no choices here
When choice would matter
Never a choice
When it would matter

You sit across from me
"Please"
I know you will go
I will never know it
Never a time I can know it
"Please" I say

Oh, I would have no place to go
I cannot hold this need I have
For you to live
"Such a fool" you say
And you smile
I regret no day I make you smile
Blind to the comedy I made for you
This blindness I could never defend
Transparent truth in your eyes
This is where I break and never bend
This need I have
For you to live

"The present life of man upon earth, O king, seems to me, in comparison with that time which is unknown to us, like to the swift flight of a sparrow through the house wherein you sit at supper in winter, with your ealdormen and thegns, while the fire blazes in the midst, and the hall is warmed, but the wintry storms of rain or snow are raging abroad. The sparrow, flying in at one door and immediately out at another, whilst he is within, is safe from the wintry tempest; but after a short space of fair weather, he immediately vanishes out of your sight, passing from winter into winter again. So this life of man appears for a little while, but of what is to follow or what went before we know nothing at all. If, therefore, this new doctrine tells us something more certain, it seems justly to deserve to be followed."
Venerable Bede's Ecclesiastical History of England, 8th Cen. AD

What makes my heart
Cannot ever leave me
Nor the soul I own
I owe to you
I see now how there's a way
In which absence creates a deeper presence
Words not heard then make their point now
I am yet stunned as to how quickly
Your eyes lost their light
How quickly the flight
So short a space
How the fire blazes in the hall
I get the point
Sitting at supper in winter
The soul I own
I owe to you

A humble journey
This flight of Life
Repeated since
Adam walked Eve
In a garden
Then
Out the Gates of Paradise
Where no day would surprise
Nor love course without hazard
Pardon
That would never work
It's all different outside Perfection
Where imperfection breeds
And like the Angels
Fallen we fall
Oh, Thy Fair Eve
Giving us the edge
Upon which Life could thrive
Where days go awry or not
And love begins blindly
This is a cursed plot
That Death segues
To Fantasy Island
I leave that story
In the mound of my grief
For I am now destroyed with a sense
Of your ending
Oh, what passage is this
That leads to a perfection
Our natures cannot bear or know
What plan is this
That turns Death
To anything good?
A humble journey
This flight of Life
When it fills with anger

Destroys the griever
Whose grief is launched
By love of you

The question that I have
Three months past your death
Is whether you are someplace
Or now only in my mind?
If there's a Heaven
You're there
Whether I go there myself
Some place I wish for
Beyond my love for you here
Doesn't come to mind
Seeing you again in some celestial realm
Is a difference I could not bear
Some progress or improvement
Beyond my love for you here
The presence of you
Was my gift in all
The Whens and Wheres
Of our Earthly Time
I'd pursue you for eternity
For a return here
But the ungratefulness of that
As if there was some greater fortune
I wished more of
Beyond my love for you here

Right now
You are in an expanse of field
Maybe a garden
Whose trees and flowers
I cannot see
Though everything blooms
As on the brightest
Glad Day Blake painted
And you are seated
Jenny pup below you
Dickens in your hands
Cissy curious
As if she alone knows
They are long dead
And no place
But every place together
This dream in which I see
You happy
With us
Your love overspilling
The fences of Death
In this dream
You never left
I cannot see
I stretch the imagining
Of these poems
Though not enough
To be with you in the brightness
Of where you are now

This is a birthday poem to Elaine
Different from all the others
Greeted by my special lady
With a look of compliance
Like a traffic ticket
Acknowledged indulgently
As a Christmas gift
You wouldn't choose
Repeated year after year
Now
You shall not be so assailed
You are where birthdays poems
Are measured quietly
For celestial worth by guardian angels
What I write now to you
Small terrestrial matters they say
I shall not argue
The special merits
Of whatever these poems convey
No more than this hope
They reach you
Different from all the others

Right now
 You're slipping away
 Quietly
I can't measure the time
From when you were here
But it is long
I didn't see it coming
Your slipping away
Before dawn
Another Christmas on the horizon
I, never to be more present
Than here
Right now
You're slipping away
Except your thoughts
I imagine are elsewhere
I can't measure the time
Or when it stopped
But it is long nonetheless
I didn't see it come
Your slipping away
Always right now
Your slipping away

I'm in this old house now
You made it beautiful
It's been bought by a stranger
A sudden meeting
We meet on the road
He doesn't seem to care
Where he goes
I won't follow
This is what emptiness looks like
Listen, I am just not able to go
Because I'm waiting
I'm in this old house now
I see in the mirror the new owner
My God
This is what emptiness looks like
But I don't tell him
Because I'm waiting

Right now, Carissima
It is inconceivable to me
That I should be here
Writing these poems
Or be anywhere
Or be doing anything
Without you
I loved you for no reason
I miss you beyond
What we ever said or did
I can present no brief
Explaining
Describing
Justifying
Why I still see
And yearn for you
What it is is so far beyond
The erudition of the mind
Or the muscle memory of the body
Mine is a grief that doesn't kill
Or seek a consigliere of the soul
I was left no option to behave
After your death
The yearning is all now
And it's enough
For you are there too

Right now, Carissima
I think there's medical cause
But no reasoning
Why you died
There's a paper trail
Explaining of what you died
But no such trail
As to what Death is
Like cataloguing the trees
While the fire still burns
Counterpunching Death
With an autopsy
Putting Death into check
With a Vegan diet
Choosing any alibi
As to why we die
Rehearsing for when
We choose not to die
Claiming the dying moment
The New Birth
Defenseless though against
Cancer's a rebel army
Oh, there is an order
Against the order we pose
Surrogates of Death
Faithful to a beginning
Of Nothing
Soldiers of The void, The Abyss
Eternity an Oblivion
Perhaps not the Devil
But an Astrophysics
Those quanta silenced, dissed, erased
By The Big Bang
Lay a finger on us
Something at the very beginning
Went angry and awry

Dead stars inhabit us angrily
So difficult to accept
Out of Nothing
Something came
A mortal stay
Box seats for humans
Mortalism our Achilles Heel
We can't shirk it off
With faith in a glorious
After-Death
I cannot go forward
Directing my own script
Choosing and willing
Something
Foolishly claim
A Will to Salvation
A Will that is Free
Or agree to an Eternal Happiness
When I object forever
That you should die
Part of the bargain

You're the proof of something
I've quite forgotten that
Two states at once
Like Schrodinger's cat
Somehow someone never brought to scale?
Or not too big to fail?
Or never there at all?
Like Shakespeare's sister?
Or Edmund's Mother?
The forgotten Pythia Oracle of Delphi?
Apollina in the shade of her brother?
Perhaps more and better
A descendent of Eve
Her act louder than the word
"The serpent me beguiled
And I did eat"
Daughters of Thy Fair Eve
You brought Eden
To human scale
And love that lives
Was born

Take this moment when someone strums
A guitar
A forgotten *faux pas*
Pricks your conscience
Certainly many
Emissaries sweep the room of consciousness
Belated finds
Patrolling for the mystery I missed
So what if friends depart or soups remain unsalted?
So what if words wander from what was
After all, your grief has gone beyond
What therapists discovered
When leaving the chicken out uncovered
So what if guests come fashionable late
No need to apologize for forgetting days
Addressing others in a purple haze
Take this moment when you speak Croat
After all your grief has gone beyond
What Freud discovered
So what at this moment
Someone sings
Patrol carefully for the hidden meaning
In Buffalo wings
My grief has gone so far beyond
All that

It's all different now
When you slip away
Not yet gone
Longer than you were here
It's all different now
The world like a body
When the breath
Of grass is gone
The tide of the Sea
Low forever
The Moon phased out
The Navigator of your soul
Gone below
It's all different now
When you slip away
Of the second I am not sure
Though an Eternity is in it
It's all different now
I feel a laughing warm breeze
Such a fool I hear you say
And I laugh too
As you slip away

Someone asks
        Are you true to her?
        And she to you?
        Or does it matter?
If what things are to me
Are not what things
Are to her?
Perhaps you say things are not
Really out there in the first place
In any way either of you can understand
As to why I am true to her
Or not really out there at all
But only the medium of God's mind
A shadow of an Ideal World
A bit of undigested potato
A working expression of what we can never understand

As to why I am true to her
Some mystery unraveling itself
Where the clock isn't running
Where what we are to each other always in process
Love a matter in itself
Time and dream
 Not matter at all
A presence in itself
Say, like a poem of flowing phrases
You cannot hold to the point
Where any question can be answered
Or words nailed to make a case
That somehow has already been made
As to why I am true to her

Why am I true to her
And what does it mean?
I'm true to her the way
The bee is true to its mission

Unknowing pollinator of our survival
The way fire licks into air it cannot reach
But feeds upon
I'm true to her like a wanderer
Who uses the moon as a beacon
I'm true to her without a compass
And true beyond where any map leads
Yet I have no grasp of the longitude and latitude
Of this dream that has made me true
Beyond what words can say
In the end I'm true to her
The way time at the beginning
Runs true to its end
And that is enough.

What is this dying
I witness
When you hold your arms straight up
Your eyes closed
To make yet one more time
That stand on your own two feet
That movement of life against gravity
You've made for seventy-two years
And three hundred and fourteen days
This dawn you can no longer make
The dying that wants you
And all our wants mean nothing

What is this dying?
Is it wiser to stoically abstain
Lean into the dying?
Take from just one piece
Of the obscenity of this ending
Take Death's pleasure
In surprising you with taking all
When you have already
Divested and want nothing?

What is this dying?
The fool fat with purchases
To take into Oblivion
But mocked by Death
Who gives only a shroud
With no pockets
Not on the trip as planned
Conceited by choices made
As if they led
To a different end

What is it this dying?
I witness

When you hold your arms straight up
Indomitable love of my life
I see at once
You've met the challenge
And done it right

When Elaine is 64
Days are going by
Too much as they were before
Too well we know their language
Where all choices end
Time gets eaten up by rote
Much happens we didn't intend
Yet I've gone out too far
Into this heady surf
Beyond any bar
Now with you

When all faces we already know
When one place is like another
Every Afterword read first
No matter one or the other
Yet I've gone out too far
Into this heady surf
Beyond any bar
Now with you

The length of summer somehow done
There when it's just begun
The path of every day is worn
What's ahead already born
Already somehow passed and done
Yet I've gone out too far
Into this heady surf
Beyond any bar
Now with you

What's between us is as real as breath
As joined as darkness to night
Invisible to the eye as far off stars
But burning as bright

What's between us has no depth
Nor breadth or fine measurement
The mesh of time together
Entangles the solid of firmament

What's between us is not speculative
No criminal charge or established intent
No injury perjury or false testimony
Nor release after so many years spent

What's between us has no sound
Sacred as words said in silence
Nor motion moving no sight seeing
No map at all to where we can be found

On this day you die
The spruce east of the house
Slashed above the power line
Where the juice runs through
Also serves the birds who roost
Lights the lamp for me
Falling asleep on too much Proust
Birds migrate sailing to Corsica on a schooner
They should have done it sooner
Some I love now dead come down the chimney
And through the walls
Through the doors and all the windows
Through the ceilings through the roof
Through the snow and down the court
On this day you die
More real than the spruce east of the house
More powerful than the power that runs its juice
Through the lines that serve the birds who roost.

The trees regain their leaf
The Moon grows full
And tides feel its pull
No App or Algorithm required
Stars live and die
Without the direction of AI
There's no need to check a phone
The Sun will rise unmessaged
No high-level coding needed
We die in the old fashioned way
A butt of humor now
The personal
The intent of poetry is not personal
As the zillion Selfies you take
But gives the feel of that casting spell
Between mind and things
Putting the thing in the word
The word in the thing
And both
By your mind's fingertips
So much like the magic
Of trees regaining their leaf
So much like the magic of a life
Of a love that masters my grief

The snow falls thin
And holds on
Enough to shovel
I pause amid
Whitened souls returning
To visit again at dusk
So I go in
Taking off my coat
I am caught by a presence:
This tree still ornamented
It's lights yellowed
So that I am infused
In other twilights
Where this same tree
Resurrected again and again
By you
Diligently
Makes the past
And those that were
Enter gently and quietly here
These whitened souls returning

All voices and faces
In this envelope of memory
So much imparted
To this flow of being
By what is not sensible
By what we pass by
But mourns and laughs
With us who think
We think the world into being
And yet what is not us
Yet holds on
And I remain fused within you
Though the snow falls thin
And holds on

There is a hidden order of things
            A secret life that binds plants to sun
            Animals to us stones to brooks
Tree to sky earth to wind fire to water
And us to it all
Every life a quest for admittance
Through invisible doors
An incantation a magical brewing
A placement of things a sequence of stars
These portals to an intertwining
Of all things and all life
A mortal tour of unknown span
Into the heart of things

You study closely to see how it works
Where the jointure of soul and mud
The tissues of blood and mind
The world our body
The trees your legs
Your voice the trees'
Stones your strength
Your movement theirs'
The stars your dreams
Your eyes theirs'
The waters your spirit
Your spirit their flow
The wind is your breath
Your breath their lungs
The animals your kin
The plants emissaries of the Sun
The sun itself your own heart
The pulse of Light
No break not a mend
No creator apart from creation
Everything that begins
Already ended

Everything that ends
At once always a beginning
Right now, Carissima